And Forward She Went

Michelee Rigdon

BookLeaf Publishing

Presentation by *BookLeaf Publishing*

Web: www.bookleafpub.com

E-mail: info@bookleafpub.com

ISBN: 9789357213547

First edition 2023

New Life

From the smoking ash,
She rises like a Phoenix,
Reborn with new strength.

Shimmering Dust

When you lose a piece of your soul, where does it go?
You spend a lifetime handing out pieces of yourself for them to be forgotten and deserted.
Do they stay drifting through life, searching for their home again?

How does one feel whole after losing so much of their being?
Life never feels the same when the flame fades out.
Spending each day trying to learn how to fill those voids is exhausting.
The constant struggle to love thyself is a never-ending testament to self-sacrifice.

One day the dark clouds clear,
The sunlight caresses your face and suddenly there is warmth flooding in.
Learning self-love is one of the hardest battles.
Keep your pieces tight and close to your heart,
They are the strength needed to find yourself.

Walking Prism

Even through the dark times,
The flame inside her flickers fiercely.
The shadows dancing freely,
Fueling the fire deeper.

The world surrounding her is monotone,
Her song is loud and vibrant.
Flowing through the grey mist like a ghost,
She leaves a trail of blinding light.

Her light shines so bright yet,
She is naive to its brilliance.
The luminescent softness makes her easily approachable,
Only the keeper of her heart knows how hard it beats.

Through the somber fields she travels,
Spreading the one beam of light she has to offer.
The world seems brighter,
When she sings her song.

Sensory Trigger

It is the scent that brings back memories of the things you try to forget the most.
It is the song that plays that reminds you of your love for music.
It is the sip of a drink or bite of food that reminds you why they were so important.

Our heart holds these things so dear because at one point in time, they were everything.
They were the reason for watching the clock at work, just ready to be in their prescence.
They were the reason your heart beat so strong you could feel it pounding in your chest.

Now the anxiety sets in when the triggers happen.
It is the heavy feeling in your chest that will not go away.
It is the sleepless nights laying and wondering.
It is the lack of appetite that makes it impossible to eat that meal again.

It is all the little things that come together.
These little things are the glue that keeps the love stuck in place.

There is no letting go of these memories, for
they created a bond between two humans.
Two humans that aimlessly found each other and
knew they never wanted to let go.

It is all of this that makes letting go so difficult.
There is a time that you have to cross that
bridge.
You have to move on to be there for yourself.
You have to stay strong and just keep going.
Learn to love the little things for the great
memories they did create because at one point,
they were all that mattered.

LOVE Living

Letting go of your fears.

Overcoming your most challenging obstacles.

Victoriously accepting your successes.

Embracing the new opportunities that await.

Quit holding yourself back and start loving all of you.

Keep Going

From struggle comes appreciation.
It can be overwhelming at times.
Enough to want to give it all up.

We reach a point where we get over the hill.
The view on the other side is breathtaking.
It is hard to keep from running in headfirst.

Instead of sprinting in blindly,
Take the time to soak in all of the experience.
Drink the waters of wisdom and bathe in the
pools of never-ending knowledge.

We get one chance each day we awake to do
something for our well-being.
Start evaluating your choices before bounding
into the unknown.
We miss important details that can save so much
pain when we go rushing through.

Take the time to learn what it is that makes you
feel complete.
Master the things that you find you love.
Do not let anyone make you feel you are
incapable of doing something.
Grab the reigns and take control.

Through the Cracks

Isn't it amazing that a seed will grow through a crack in the concrete?
A tiny pit,
Capable of life in an instant.

It takes time to germinate.
The life slowly comes creeping from the shell.
Seeking sustenance,
Growing a little more as time carries on.

The seedling reaches it's roots deep in the soil.
Soaking in the nutrients from the earth.
Spreading like veins,
Gaining strength.

For years these trees grow stronger,
The rings of life grow thicker.
The flora lush,
Bearing fruits of new life.

The cycle continues,
Nature pollinates the earth.
The air is thick,
Pollen dust settling everywhere.

The stages of life are similar all around,
We all bleed in some form.
We breathe some type of breath,
Reaching for something.

It takes time and patience to nourish a seed,
To watch it's delicate flowers blossom,
It's sweet fruits plumping.
Bask in the serenity of growth.

A spec

A spec so small.
So miniscule.
So minute.

A spec floating in an abyss of stars.
Burning all around.
Vibrant and bright.

A spec amongst a plethora of other specs.
Each significantly unique.
Aimlessly existing.

Serotonin

The rush floods in like a strong wave,
Coursing and churning,
Filling in all of the cracks.

The intensity surges through the nervous system,
the receptors arcing and snapping,
Waking up the deepest pits inside.

The gears start turning,
Creaking and grinding,
Sending the serotonin through the twists and
turns.

It feels like soaring,
Drifting and floating,
Unable to slow it down.

Is it too much for people?
Do they notice the struggle?
All of this,
Just to share a smile?

Star Gazer

She is lost in the vast darkness.
So dark,
It cuts out the rest of the world around.

It is her and the sky now.
She drifts,
Losing herself within the deep blanket.

The sky glittering with burning dust.
Small fragments,
Burning up with trailing tails.

She dances on the planet's rings.
So gingerly,
Each step is her display of affection.

Her devotion to the Moon,
So innocent,
She shares her gratitude in her song.

Her melody reaches to the farthest corners.
So pure,
She bleeds her heart into each verse.

She travels onward into the universe.
Freely fearless,
She sends her message all along.

Winter's Kiss

The cold rushes in,
Blanketing the world in silence.

The stillness is heavy,
Too heavy to put into words.

The quiet so thick,
It can be cut with a blade.

The days are shorter,
Leaving no time for sunlight.

The trees shed their foliage,
Leaving the branches bare and cold.

The creatures seek shelter,
Running from the shivering touch of frost.

It is time for the earth to rest,
In order to make way for new life.

Spring Blossom

The thick winter slowly melts away,
Leaving the earth beneath exposed.

The earth is moist and crawling with life,
The world is beginning to wake up again.

Slowly the blades of grass push through soil,
Thickening by the days.

The trees begin to bloom,
Bearing new fruits of life.

The birds return to perch upon the branches,
Singing their songs of joy.

The world slowly becomes brighter,
Leaving the bleek winter grey behind.

New life is born all around,
Filling the trees with movement.

Slowly the dreary winter days melt away,
Awakening a new beginning of fresh breath.

Summer Breeze

Each day is longer,
Crawling through the hours slowly.

The warmth of the sunlight floods in,
Filling every crack and pore.

The winter grey that set in,
Lifts and disappears into the morning dew.

The air is hot and loud with the sound of creatures,
Buzzing and chirping a variety of song.

The stars seem brighter at night,
Laying and getting lost in the sky.

Summer night breezes flow by,
Carrying the smell of grass and flowers.

Still warm from soaking in the sun all day,
Sleep comes easy with the sounds of summer.

Autumn Leaves

The crisp air is thick with earth,
Ground crunching beneath foot.

The smell of harvest is heavy,
Trees bursting with fresh fruits.

The colors are so vibrant,
Green to red to orange.

The autumn breeze is brisk,
Clutching a sweater a little tighter.

Autumn brings reflection of light,
Before the world gets dark again.

The turtle and the rat

Is it strange to see these two together,
A tiny rat and a hardened turtle.
Drifting through the days in sync.

The rat is sleek,
Cunning and wise.
Quick to jump though.

The turtle is smug,
Thoughtful and reserved.
Quick to get lost though.

The rat moves fast,
Rapid and blunt,
No time to think.

The turtle thinks,
Meticulously and deeply.
Each move carefully planned.

Is it destiny to see these two,
Side by side.
Taking on the challenges of life.

The rat protects the turtle,
Wholeheartedly and passionately.
Nothing stops the bleeding hearts.

Fate had entwined them together,
Tangled and knotted.
Their souls bonded tightly forever.

Wildflower

Tiny and purple.
Swaying softly in the breeze.
Bees dance upon the petals.
Butterflies kiss the sweet nectar.
Sunlight warms it's face.
It's blossoms are so vibrant.
The fields are speckled for miles.

Sweet wildflower dancing.
Digging its roots deep.
Spreading its love into the earth.
Sharing its sweet scent with the breeze.
Capturing the warmth of summer.
Pollinating the field around.
Sharing sustenance for new life.

Intensity

It is not handled by people well.
Raw brutal honesty.
In your face truth.

People are fearful if it.
They can not bear to deal with facts.
No matter how much proof there is.

Intensity is a strength.
It keeps you lifted.
It gives you motivation.

There are things in this life that we strive to reach.
Hardwork must be put forth.
Leaving you with success.

Stay soft, but be hardened.
Stay wise, but be humble.
Stay quiet, but be willing to speak up.

Infinite

Limitless.
There are no obstacles that can stop motivation.

Fearless.
There is no storm able to conquer the thirst for the sea.

Immeasurable.
There is no length too long to travel when a heart's desire is at the end.

Infinite.
There is no amount of time that is set for a goal to be met.

If it takes years to achieve,
It is still worth it.
There is an infinite amount of energy,
With a large amount of work to be done.

Raw

Scarred from the past,
Wounds are visible upon the surface.

Each telling a tale,
Of trauma's kiss.

The stain is hidden,
Deep in the past.

It is never too far,
Still within reach at a moment's notice.

A memory can be a haunting thing,
Flooding in feelings that have been buried for years.

There is still fight in her,
She still stands tall.

She battles each day,
Head on.

There is nothing that can stop her,
For her willpower is too strong.

Stronger than the mightiest ocean,
Stronger than the harshest winds.

She keeps pushing through it,
Because she must.

All along

Motion sickness heavy.
Once that feeling starts it hits like a wave.
Powerful and overwhelming.
Too strong to fight.

It just keeps surging.
No end in sight.
The fear of no end rises.
Like being on a sinking ship.

The mind races.
Quick and scurried.
It is hard to find a stable mindset.
Worry is washing over and over.

All along it is just someone else's anxiety.
All along it is a pressure that is unable to be stabilized.
All along the heart raced and churned with hit blood.
But all along it ended up being ok.
All along it was just a thought.
All along it was never real.

The End

Is it the end?
Or is this a new beginning?

A door has closed,
But there is another side to the it.
A portal to a new dimension,
Something fresh.

It may feel like the world is collapsing in when you close that door,
But did you shut it just in time?
Perhaps sparing the sight of past's ruins.

It is not easy to start fresh,
Innocent to the new surroundings.
What better time to soak in the knowledge around,
Learning new things you never thought to try.

It does not hurt to learn something new,
It helps to keep the mind strong.
People tend to worry about their physical appearance, but never their mind's strength.

Keep stretching your limits,
Farther than you thought you were capable of.
Feel the burst of energy and prepare for any
obstacles that may come up.

There is always another door.
Another end.
Another new beginning.

www.ingramcontent.com/pod-product-compliance
Lightning Source LLC
Chambersburg PA
CBHW051717130826
49812CB00034B/1220
9789357213547